PRAISE FO

Even though I am a poet, I often have difficulty understanding a poem, discerning the meaning. One of the many things I appreciate about *Home Coming* is that the poems are not veiled, the meaning is not obscured. In Albers'writing, there is both an immediate impact with pointed clarity, and then layers of personal response that roll out. This collection is both wickedly funny and heartbreakingly relevant. I will come to these pages often. It is a collection of verse relevant for our tumultuous times.

– **Mary Anne em Radmacher, Author of *Live with Intention*, Aphorist, Artist, Poet**

This book is a meditation on modern life by a writer not afraid to speak her truth, which in itself is an invitation for all of us to do the same. In it, Caren Albers offers her perspective on painful topics like the divisiveness of politics, the introspection caused by COVID-19 sheltering-in-place, the destruction of both hurricanes and cancer, and—beyond all that—the glimmers of hope we all need to survive. Her sharp wit keeps this collection of poetry and prose from being too dark, but in all honesty, it is the most poignant and meaningful when the humor is left behind and what remains is a sheer human vulnerability with which we can all identify.

– **Patti Digh, Author of *Life is a Verb* and seven other books**

A beautiful blend of sass and sentiment! From humor to heartache and back again, Caren reminds us that we can navigate even the thorniest brambles with "rock solid bonds and tender love."

– **Sue Ann Gleason, Writer, Poet, Coach**

Caren shares that this book was written to keep her sane, grounded, and uplifted through the year that was 2020. In the prologue, she poses the question "What happens when the winds blow, the ground shakes, and you lose your proverbial footing?" The answer, if you are the nimble-spirited, generously humorous, compassionately frank and thereby rollickingly resilient kind of creative like Caren Albers, is you go right ahead and feel that ground shaking and turn that lost footing into a dance! Something about the candor, the heart, and the easy-ness with which Caren choreographs ideas, images, and words, makes it effortless to fall into rhythm with her prose. It's important to notice the good that can come from challenging times. Creatives like Caren remind us of that. I'm grateful for Caren for having wrought the light and levity that is *Home Coming.*

– **Leah Campbell-Badertscher, J.D., Artist, Writer, Master Coach, Founder of The Art School & Renascence Co.**

Caren Albers is the kind of writer whose work can stir you to laugh to keep from crying — or cry from laughing too hard. Author Ram Dass famously said, "We're all just walking each other home." Albers' *Home Coming* offers a revealing look at her personal journey.

– **Cathryn Castle Garcia, Author, *Ocean Metaphor: Unexpected Life Lessons from the Sea***

Bold and unapologetic, like your favorite aunt who just doesn't care what others think anymore...she says it like it is and you both expect it and delight in it. *Home Coming* is a welcome, artful pause in the ordinary...and a vivid exploration of our current unbeckoned, collective extraordinary. Albers shares a truly reverent treatment of the irreverent, reminding readers of the absolute certainty of the one constant right now...absolute uncertainty. All these things with shock, awe, and raw honesty. Perhaps many more collections of thought-provoking, original poetry would be devoured by meaning-seekers if they included the words "batshit crazy" and references to Magic 8 Balls. Until then, we have this timely and timeless reminder that poetry has the power and the pull to open our eyes, our minds, our hearts to the possible, even as we navigate stunning and heart wrenching challenges in our actual. *Home Coming* lives up to Albers' realization (or perhaps revelation) that "The poem remembers a simpler time. Finding contrast with harder ones, too." A buffet of food for thought...and a welcome feast for the soul.

– **Deanna Davis PhD, Author of *Laugh, Cry, Eat Some Pie*, CEO Applied Insight, LLC**

Home Coming is filled with poignant, heartbreaking moments, right alongside sharp-witted, funny moments; just like life. That's what is captured among *Home Coming's* poems and essays, life as it is, imperfect, infuriating, unfair, glorious, funny, and filled with love. Caren Albers shares all these aspects of life with an honest eye and a thoughtful, often laugh-provoking, turn of phrase.

– **Lynda Allen, Poet, Artist, Author of three poetry collections: *Rest in the Knowing, Illumine, Wild Divinity,* the nonfiction spiritual guidebook, *The Rules of Creation*, and the novel, *Sight to See***

Home Coming is Caren Albers raw, seriously honest, sometimes funny, spot on account of politics, the pandemic and personal devastation. Through poetry and prose, Albers recounts what it's like to be a small blue dot in a big red field, in a county where 70% of her neighbors voted for the other guy. She generously invites us into the very personal world of cancer and tight family, and shows us what happens when Covid-19 comes to town, and Trump starts tweeting and her neighbors respond with lawn signs and MAGA hats. These beautifully honest poems instruct us on what it means to grapple with being a neighbor, a human being, and a loving family member in a time of division, heartbreak and stress. *Home Coming* is a personal narrative, written with love and care. The bright lights are everywhere. It's a book about survival.

– **Laurie Marks Wagner, Creator of 27 Powers, Writing Teacher, Coach, author of 7 books**

In *Home Coming – Belonging and Knowing*, author Caren Albers poetically delivers smart, soul-ish, and wise words on politics, pandemic life, and what it takes to be the supportive, sassy, resilient spouse of a cancer survivor. Reading Albers' book is like taking a brisk walk with a trusted old friend, where words fly and time doesn't exist. She shares her path of discovering that it's OK to just be yourself, with her "all in" attitude. As you walk alongside her the knowing of what it takes to save ourselves becomes clear. I understood what she meant with: "It took an ocean of tears to learn how to save myself, to learn that the CPR I needed had to come from me...that I am loved JUST AS I AM." This is a book for all of us who've ever wondered who we are and if we are enough to get from the beginning of life to the end intact. Maybe even more than intact but glad we took the journey. You'll keep coming back to her words to remind yourself to stay "all in" in your own life.

– **Jeanette Richardson Herring, Poet, Author of *The Dust of Shooting Stars***

HOME COMING

Home Coming

Belonging and Knowing

Caren Albers

Heart Irony Publishing

Published by Heart Irony Publishing

Cover Design and Layout: Caren Albers
Interior Formatting by Euan Monaghan, StandOut Books

Home Coming - Belonging and Knowing

ISBN (print): 978-1-7366821-0-4
ISBN (ebook): 978-1-7366821-1-1

Printed in the United States of America

TABLE OF CONTENTS

PART 1: POLITICS

PART 2: PANDEMIC

PART 3: PERSONAL HURRICANES

PART 4: PATHWAYS

THE POEM OF ME

Sassy Sage
Wisecracking Warrior
Grand-Darling Spoiler
Vegan Husband Lover
Baby Mother
Funny Bunny
Happy Honey
Sane but Crazy
Never Lazy
Truth-Teller
Artful Dweller
Soulful Friend
Until the End

HOME COMING DANCE

I have come to dance.
Not the barely moving my feet dance
or the shaking my arms dance.
The shaking all over dance.
The dance that wakes everything
leaving nothing to the imagination dance.
The naked truth dance.
The mother daughter dance.
The word dance.
The says everything
at all costs dance.

The ugly cry snot dance.
The stamping, "I didn't get my way" dance.
The dance that insists, "No, you sit down,
I dance alone" dance.
The "I don't want you" dance.
The dance of fools dance.
The "you're not clever" dance.
The "I don't like you" dance.
The "I don't have time for your shit" dance.
The not interested in your shit dance.

The "go away" dance,
The "get lost" dance.
I have come to dance

however the hell I want to dance.
The "none of your business" dance.
The saving me from stupidity
and all things stupid dance.
Like a force to be reckoned with dance.
Like a "fuck you and the horse you road in on" dance.
Like we are fresh out of compassion
and serving only shade today dance.

I have come to celebrate
the things that will change,
things that will end,
things that will fall apart,
and the things that will be put back together dance.

Always dancing like someone's watching,
like it matters,
like a freight train that can't be stopped.
I have come to dance feet flying in the air.
People wondering if I'm crazy or just half crazy.

I have come to dance
Don't try to stop me or direct me
or tell me how you think I should dance.

I have come to dance,
not for you.

For me.

PROLOGUE

What happens when the winds blow and the ground shakes and you lose your proverbial footing? When yesterday feels so far away and today overflows with new things, things you never dreamed would happen?

Home Coming is a book of poems and essays about surviving, storms, pandemics, politics, personal hurricanes, memories, mothers, and other misadventures.

I fancy the writing smart, entertaining, truthful, hopeful, and funny. I hope you do, too. It reflects a deep dive into that special place of knowing and belonging we all have.

Politics – Because Politics affects everything, I start there. Full disclosure, I cried every day for six weeks after the 2016 election resulting in the presidency of Donald J. Trump. I understand firsthand what the losing side of the 2020 election feels like. I believed strongly in my values and that the policies of the incoming administration would cause devastating changes. I write about what it's like to be a small blue dot in a big red field. In my county, 71% voted Republican. I bend toward irony; in fact, I never met an irony I didn't love. Cosmic irony is one of my favorites. If reading about politics bothers you, don't worry it's a short section.

Pandemic – Well, then along came Covid-19, our quickest lesson in changing the world forever. Sadly, Trump and Covid-19 proved to be comorbidities. Facing the biggest crisis of our lifetime, a lack of leadership prevailed. The nation split further into reds and blues and blacks, browns, and whites. Mask wearing became a political statement that put people's lives in jeopardy. The nation was led by tweets, over 15,000 and counting. Covfefe that?

Personal Hurricanes – Apparently, Michael, a CAT 5 Hurricane that hit us here in Panama City, Florida on October, 10, 2018, wasn't enough. Around the corner, a few personal hurricanes waited. Two days before Michael hit, my beloved mother-in-law was diagnosed with a brain tumor and died within two months. The day after his mother died, my husband Bob received his own Cancer diagnosis, delayed weeks by the devastation of buildings and infrastructure that included doctors' offices not having working phones lines for months after the hurricane. Thus began our arduous journey of healing and a rediscovery of the rock solid bond and tender love of our forty year marriage.

Pathways – None of us travel a straight line, do we? We zig and we zag and often backtrack. At the intersections of our lives, we meet people who play important roles in discovering our true selves and finding our way home. So much history goes into who we are and how we got there. In the last section of poems and essays, you'll get a taste of the twists and turns in my life shared from my open heart, often with lots of humor.

PART ONE

Politics

FAT BUNNIES

I live in a dinky town with a Trump Store.
A confederate flag proudly hangs in the window.
I've tried snapping photos of it from the intersection.
But they always turn out distorted and blurry.

I've considered pulling into the parking lot
for closer view. But I don't.
I fear I couldn't stifle the urge to go in and ask
"Are the Confederate flags flammable?"

This morning at 6 am I decide
Today is the day I'll start walking again.
I grab yesterday's clothes which in reality are the day before's, too
and tiptoe out of the bedroom.

The sun is rising as I start walking on the bike path across from my
house.
A large bunny with floppy ears runs across the path.
It's not a frightened, stringy, street bunny.
It's a fat bunny, for sure someone's pet.

Then I see its accomplice,
A champagne-colored bunny with a black and white circle around
one eye.
Neither looks like they have ever missed a meal in their lives.
"What are y'all doing?" I say in my locally acquired vernacular.

I walk on until I reach the house that looks like a Trump
compound.
A less cultured person might call it a "shithole shack."
American flags and Trump signs line the overgrown driveway and
hang overhead.
"Promises Made Promises Kept" catches my eye.

I decide that's far enough for today, turn around, and head home.
The fat bunnies are now nuzzled comfortably close to a house.
They know where they live.
And so do I.

SIDE EFFECTS MAY INCLUDE EUPHORIA

Tired is the gift that keeps on giving
Sweet, lingering exhaustion, energy spent
Physical or mental, good or bad.

Yesterday, I dog sat for Rosie, my son's girlfriend's puppy
Puppies are like babies
You have to watch them every minute.

Anticipate, anticipate, anticipate
What do you need?
Tell me. In, out, up, down. I'll do it. hah hah hah

Pets provide doses of the good Oxy,
Oxytocin the cuddle hormone secreted by the Pituitary,
A small pea-sized gland at the base of the brain.

I figure the "Intelligent Designer"
Realizing how complex the brain turned out
Threw in oxytocin to avoid constant emotional crash landings.

Oxycontin, the addictive opioid, Oxy,
Oxy, moron, two words, Rush Limbaugh
Medal of Freedom winner my ass,
Preferred drug of choice after ignorance and hate.
Ignorance and hate harder to kick than Oxy.

Rosie leaped into my lap in a single bound all day long
Knocking me over in more ways than one.

Poor Rosie missed her mommy and so did I.
Tux really hated the resident alien's friendly takeover
Welcoming her 9 pm departure.

The mommy and puppy reunion was epic
Like videos of soldiers returning from years at war.

Me, I was tired. Bone tired
With a full tank of Oxy.
The good kind!

SHOVELS DOWN

When I was raised, we were taught it wasn't polite to bring up religion or politics in a social setting. Also, the only thing we could be sure of was death and taxes. I'm starting to see the wisdom in that.

In the sixties, I can't even imagine how long it would take for a theory or idea of any kind to create a groundswell and a following. News was only on television three times a day for a half hour.

The pace at which information flows today is astounding. Within minutes there are social media posts and tweets and retweets about almost everything. I could probably trace back and do an entire historical article about how we got here. I'm sure you could, too. But that's not what I'm most interested in. What I want to know is how do we get out of here?

How do we go back to a time when everything about us wasn't assumed, scripted, or assigned by our political party affiliation? We are better than that. How do we learn how to listen again? How can we wrestle "the certainty" from our cold dead hands? Hyperbole intended! Yes, I'm afraid it will take that.

It's like we live in parallel universes. The conservative party has its own news outlets that create the reality of their news. The liberal factions of the media also decide what to get that side all frothed up about. Maybe we should take a step back and realize how we are all being used in this game.

I want to build a time machine and go back to the 1970s. Not that politics or anything else was perfect then, but discussions were about differences of opinion and debated on merit. Opinions could get heated, but rarely violent. A strong sense of decorum existed in the highest offices. Violence viewed as immature and inappropriate. Over the years somehow decorum has been eroded.

We seem to get triggered and strike back instinctively. Possibly some of my poems have already triggered or will trigger you. I hope you'll keep reading because I'm so much more than my political views and so are you.

We are all valuable humans sharing space on a spinning orb rotating around the sun or at least that's what I believe. We need to reestablish a culture where friends can disagree with each other politically and still remain friends. We'd be lying if we didn't admit that is hard right now and heartbreaking.

I don't have all the answers or a time machine. My hope is that we see each other's humanity before it's too late. That obstruction and division are no longer a rallying cry or our business as usual stance. That we commit to solving the problem. Otherwise, we are just digging a bigger hole.

The hole is deep enough.

Let's put our shovels down.

AWAKE

Today, I couldn't resist the siren song of cable news.
By evening, I'm awash with election anxiety.
I head to bed early. TV remote out of reach.
I relax into my own thoughts, words, and writing.
Determined to invite back my good friend, sleep.

All day Tuesday, I thought it was Monday.
Nights awake at 2 am 3 am 4 am.
Disruption best describes the last seven months.
No end in sight, with escalating anxiousness.

When I wake up, I hold my eyes tightly closed.
Allowing no light to penetrate.
Listening for the faint sound of cars passing by.
Waiting for my signal, a new day dawned.

Lying there, I remember last night's dream.
A family Christmas gathering pushed to January.
Sitting in a circle realizing no one brought food.
Leaving to buy some. I suggest potato soup.
"Milk is bad for you" someone yells loudly.
"Oh it's January!" I say. "Health kicks and New Year's resolutions."

Awake, I wonder what will happen next January.
Will we be bombarded with diets and gym commercials?
Or will we remain obsessed with simply trying to stay alive?

If the candidate who believes in herd immunity wins,
Will more of our most vulnerable be sick and dying?
Will kids grow up absent the unconditional love of grandparents?

I finally open my eyes.
The clock reads 6 am.
"Mission Accomplished!"
Outside my window,
I see the tree I trimmed yesterday.
Lower branches carefully cut.
Offering just a glimpse
of what's beyond.

NO WINNERS

The president has the coronavirus.
The man who denounced mask wearing.
Who scoffed at social distancing.
Who equated wearing a mask with weakness,
or worse, being a Democrat.
The man who just the night before at a rally,
already showing symptoms,
said the virus is rounding the corner and will be gone soon.
The man who disagreed with his own health experts.
The man who encouraged others to deny the science.
The man who claimed the coronavirus was a hoax.
Compassion does not celebrate but the irony is not lost.

Some people have to touch a hot stove to learn.
Some people never learn.

I watch all day the thing I'd sworn off, TV news.
In the morning, they say "he has no symptoms."
By noon "he has mild symptoms."
During the day he received an antiviral cocktail.
By dinner, he's boarding a helicopter for Walter Reed Hospital.
Everyone wearing masks, including President Trump.
The man who travels in superlatives everywhere he goes,
"The Best, Most Amazing, Most Perfect, No One Better,"
releases a short video as the helicopter flies off.
He says "I think I'm doing very well."

As the evening progresses more dominoes fall.
Several around the president test positive.
Many of them his surrogates.
Many who dealt in half truths, lies, and conspiracy theories.
Casting doubt, calling everyone else "fake news."
Surrogates that helped him divide our country.
Even in something as simple as mask wearing.
Surrogates who support his "It is what it is" statement.
Referring to over 200,000 Americans killed by the virus.
Surrogates who will cross any line in support of him.
Compassion does not celebrate but the irony is not lost.

I wake up in the middle of the night afraid to look at the news, afraid for our country.
Tears betray my eyes for all the chaos and sadness of the last four years.
For all the damaged institutions and threats to our democracy.
For the dog whistles and fires of racism stoked daily.
But mostly, I cry for the families divided and friendships splintered.
Compassion does not celebrate but the irony is not lost.

There are no winners here.

I NEED TO KNOW

Listen hard.
Today is different.
And today is the same.

It's hard to say thank you for the rich getting richer and the poor getting poorer.

It's hard to believe secret, government-backed police are brutally attacking citizens exercising their right to protest in America.

It's hard to say thank you for an unqualified president who stokes racism and encourages people's shadow side to make himself look better.

It's hard to say thank you for the isolation from friends and family trapped in a political climate of polarization trying their best not to catch Covid-19.

It's easy to say thank you for all my blessings, for financial security, for beautiful vistas outside my window, for enough to enjoy and some to share.

It's easy to say thank you for family that so far remains untouched by the virus except for a distant cousin who I probably wouldn't recognize on the street.

It's easy to say thank you for political winds blowing that indicate, according to polls, this nightmare will end in November. At the same time, it's hard to believe that, too.

But I simply must believe because how much uncertainty can a person carry before they fall down, fall over, fall apart, fall to their knees, or fall into a directionless heap?

Listen hard.
How much?
I need to know.

I'VE STOPPED PRETENDING...

That it's the polarization of politics, not the people, who are the problem.
That I can be friends with anyone who rationalizes putting kids in cages.
That trafficking in conspiracy theories is anything but batshit crazy.
That blind devotion to political cults or any cults can ever end well.
That single issue voters care about anything but One. Single. Issue.
That our democracy will be okay.

Nothing to see here.
So much to say here.
Because it's over...
I have stopped pretending.

OUT OF THE BLUE

Thanks for driving up
my 40 foot wooded driveway.
For getting out of your truck
to introduce yourself.
For telling me
you appreciate my Biden/Harris sign.
Especially, the installation,
safely up in the tree.

That you are my neighbor
a mile down the road matters.
That you took the risk
and time to reach out matters.

I am a tiny blue dot
in a field of red
as far as the eye can see.
In politics before,
we had differences,
but we respected them.
At home, we might say
the other side was crazy.
But unless cornered at a cocktail party
we kept our opinions to ourselves
and voted our conscience.
That was before we got divided

into MAGA hats
and everyone else.

When people cared
more about each other
than political ideology.
Yesterday, I worried the repair guy
wouldn't show because of my sign.
And then you,
my beautiful ally,
my new friend,
stopped by out of the blue.

You can't imagine
what your visit meant to me.
As the election draws near,
I have trouble breathing.
The stakes are so high;
Respect and truth are on trial.

Thank you for sharing
your light in my world.
For showing up
to let me know
I am not alone.
For the smile of surprise
your openness delivered.
For caring about
a Biden/Harris victory.

It's like watching a movie
and waiting to see if truth wins.
But now, I know,
we are watching the movie
TOGETHER.

ABOUT THIS POEM

It's hard to imagine what it's like to be a small blue dot in a big red field, in a county that votes 70% Republican. I write poems about it. I work hard to reconcile how isolated I feel. How anxious I am to get back to a time when our politics don't define us—how we treat others does. Not divided into MAGA hats and everyone else. Back to a time of respectable dialogue on both sides. As the election approaches, each day feels harder and harder because the stakes feel so high. Truth is on trial. I never understood why "thou shall not lie" needed to be a commandment until 2020. Now I do.

THANKS GIVING

For the cranberry sauce, the stuffing and gravy.
For the Covid that's driving all of us crazy.
For the tray tables that will be six feet spaced.
For son and grands outside saying grace.
For the sun and moon in all of their phases.
For my grateful heart traveling places.
For those I'm with and those I can't see.
May both of our days feel happy and free.

Cheers to old friends and new friends.
Better days around the next bend.
Giving thanks to one and to all.
2020 nears its curtain call.
No longer do I give it "the finger."
Thanks to Covid-19, Trump won't linger.
2020 so much to hate.
But you did come through
Before it was too late.

PART 2

Pandemic

PANDEMIC MEMOIR - CHAPTER 1

Today, without a single warning, my toenail fell off. One minute it's a perfectly good toenail and the next it's lifting up, hanging by a thread exposing a raw underbelly. I call Bob over to take a look. I don't know why except maybe weird things need a witness.

He immediately starts on a rant about how I must have gotten a fungus at the nail salon, which by the way shows relaxing spa videos and uses throw away plastic liners in their feet sinks. I feel it would be remiss for us not to consider "common questionable cause fallacy" (A + B are regularly associated but no third common cause is looked for therefore A is the cause of B). If memory serves me from my college logic class, that's it.

Conspiracy theories aside, since childhood I have stubbed my toes, broken my toes, dropped things on my toes and on and on. Overnight, I wake up wondering "What if Bob is right?" He is the official one in charge of "worry" in our relationship, and probably has kept me alive a time or two.

What if I have a fungus? YIKES! What if I get really sick with a systemic infection and need to go to the doctor? We've been totally self-isolating for Covid19 for 8 weeks. I can't die of toe fungus. That would be so embarrassing. Who would ever have thought we'd live in a time when we were afraid to go to the doctor? None of us, except maybe Bill Gates.

In early March, as I traveled back from a Mandala workshop in Sarasota with my art friends, the news was finally starting to sink in. Covid19 was coming and lots of people would die. Bob begged me to be careful in the airport and cancel two trips I had planned in the coming weeks.

Covid-19, with its crippling uncertainty, was lurking around the next corner. There was one thing we knew for certain, we sure as hell better have enough toilet paper. No one mentioned tampons. They rarely do.

MAGIC 8 BALL

It was not on the map.
Not in the tour book.
Not on anyone's radar.
Just beyond the billowing curtain
Uncharted waters appeared.
The page on the wall calendar.
Months behind.
Stuck on March, 2020.
No one had any real answers.
The only thing certain was uncertainty.
The best the Magic 8 Ball could do was "Ask again later."
So I'm waiting...

FOR THE GREATER GOOD

I like my Mexican Petunias neatly trimmed.
Their nature is invasive and wild.
But today, my heart wouldn't let me cut them
For fear of disappointing the butterflies.

Would they accept the loss and move on?
Would they act like petulant teens
Believing I ruined their lives on purpose?
Today, I couldn't risk it.

I wasn't prepared for this dichotomy
For Covid-19 to become
A battle of them versus me.

I'm not crying "Wolf"
The same statistics we all see
Yet your conclusions always different.

Masks usually hide things
But today, they reveal
Things I don't want to see.
I was willing to save you.
But you weren't willing to save me.

I know a year seems
Like an eternity

But death is the only finality.

"Life changing" a new meaning now,
None untouched, unscathed, unscarred.

When this is over
I will neaten my space.
Prune away all invasive outliers.

And yes, I will flourish again.
Trusting once more in the great wide open

...Unless things go south,
Then all bets are off.

I WANT TO TELL YOU

It's like nothing I've ever imagined. I wasn't one of those who watched science fiction. I didn't imagine a world so foreign. I didn't believe in zombies and now I start to wonder what else might be true.

I want to tell you that I was nearly a thousand miles away from my 85 year old mom and really the number of miles doesn't matter because even if I was close by, I probably would have chosen to let my brother alone care for her because I would worry I was a silent carrier and could cause her to die.

I want to tell you that it's so very weird not walking into a single store. I've been at home for five weeks tomorrow and it feels like so much more. Not having a schedule of things I must do, places I must go, sometimes makes everyday feel like all the rest.

I want to tell you that this time with my husband is special. I find myself responding to him tenderly where in the past I might have been snappish. Thinking he needed to get with the program or is he asking me that again. Now we are each other's lifelines and his life just as precious as my own.

I want to tell you that Covid-19 is in everything. It's like elevator music playing in the background of my life. I rarely think of anything that I don't see through that lens. Will the government make the right decisions? Will we have the food we want? I feel bad writing that. It shows my privilege and my heartaches for others who I know struggle.

I want to tell you about the man I saw coming out of the thicket in the undeveloped woody lot beside the golf course. He pushed a bike and yawned, seemingly ready to face the day. I wondered how he ended up there. How hard his life must be. How hard it must be to crawl in and out of the shadows each night.

I want to tell you how sad it makes me feel to see my son, his fiancé, and my grands and only look at them, careful not to penetrate the safety of our distance. I imagine what it might feel like to be dead in another realm and see people but not be with them. I truly hope there is none of that after we die because it hurts and I don't like hurting.

I want to tell you that we will be better spouses, better grandparents, better friends, better people, and I hope a better world because of this pause. Loss will teach us not to take people and things for granted. It's a BIG wish but I hope it comes true.

I want to tell you that when life gets back to a normal, when we go into the next phase of whatever this is going to be, I may hug the little ones so tight they scream. I may see myself and the world differently as having stopped for this brief time when a lot of people weren't as lucky as me and got off the ride and went on to what is next.

I'll see differently, love differently, act differently, and my heart will ache some for all the sacrifices of the world.

I want to tell you that I was a little glad when some of the things I had on my schedule became impossible to do. There are things I won't go back to, things that will be left behind. When all is said and done, I hope I remember my commitment to that.

CURRENT FOREVER

In some ways I'm coasting,
canceling plans,
waiting for better thoughts.

I can pick things up with my toes.
I possess an uncanny knack
for catching things thrown to me.
It's not lost on me
my need to be right is "poof" gone.

I stand all alone in the spot
between light and the dark
where humor lives.

Our right minds know "forever"
is a figment of our imagination.
Yet we hold tightly to it, believing in it.
That is until our current "forever" ends.

WHERE THE REAL WORK BEGINS

We like to know the beginning, middle, and end before we start something. Where is the fun in that? It takes away the reason to get up every day and discover things like "what is in this very moment."

My 86 year old mother has memory issues and I adore the serious look on her face when we video chat and she is trying to come up with an answer, a memory. Because for her just afterward she gets this extremely peaceful "Oh well" look on her face and we both laugh. Humor connects us. A life void of sarcasm is not a life worth living; she would agree when she can remember.

In many ways, our work has just begun, three months plus into living with the dangers of COVID-19. Well, some of us see it that way. Others are having their rights infringed on. I want to say/yell at them, "The world promises you NOTHING, nothing hear me!" Until someone you love almost dies, you might not understand. You might miss the lesson that like it or not "what is, IS!"

You will probably never fully recover the idea that life works out all the time. You've stepped too close to an edge, you can never unsee or unfeel. You can't go back to who you were, how you were. None of us can.

So the real work continues. You entertain thoughts you don't want to have because if you try to stop them, they linger and do more damage. You've learned to let them blow through like a hurricane and clean up after.

Last week, I walked down the stairs gazing at the beauty outside thinking "someday I'll be doing this alone." I have no reason to think this. Except for all that time spent looking over that edge trying not to fall in and realizing still the work goes on.

CHANGE

My Metta Meditation for loving kindness has been edited.
It used to begin:
May I be peaceful.
May I be happy.
May my heart be open.

"Happy" did not make the cut.
"Healthy" has taken her place.

May I be peaceful.
May I be healthy.
May my heart be open.

I work hard for my heart to remain open.
And now with Covid-19, hard to remain healthy.
"Happy" will mount a successful comeback some day.

Until she does, I'll deal with burning facts.
Daily pressures building beyond capacity.
Stinging truths spilling colorless liquid from my eyes.

"Happy" and I share a long history.
She is connected to my strong past.
She believes wholeheartedly in my bright future.
And even when I can't see her,
I always know she's smiling at me.

OKAY BOOMER

I'm a Boomer born after World War II
Prosperity paced forward
Home ownership the new American dream
GI Bill, families, religion

Cold War my childhood enemy
Drills, sirens, safety under desks
Our answer to Russia's threats
Bombs, radiation, devastation

Vietnam War our revolution
Drop out, be in, peace
I'm a Boomer living in the scourge of a pandemic
Expendable, invisible, forgotten

Generations X, Y, Z, M, and C
Come after me
Russia still a threat
Sabotage, influence, elections

Is Covid-19 the new enemy?
Or is it stupidity?
Or science denying
Or political dividing
Or for all of the above, choose (E)

Take your time
None of us are going
Anywhere safely,
Anytime soon...

Unless it's on Zoom

ABOUT THIS POEM

I remember so vividly the Cold War days. The drills where the siren sounded and we were instructed to climb under our desks for safety. That was a defining thing for children born in the fifties and sixties. I started to wonder if Covid-19 would be the defining factor for today's children, their Cold War. Russia is still the enemy but threatening us in different ways like interfering in our elections. In today's political climate a large swath of Americans refuse to believe it. Unlike during the Cold War, right now we are a country divided with no agreed upon enemy except maybe each other.

LOWERING THE BAR

I'm not attempting anything Herculean.
Not going to "Tap-Fit"
or get a "Beach Body."
Not learning a new language
or how to play the piano.

Not giving up sugar
or caffeine or alcohol.
I'm not giving up anything.
I've given up enough already.

I'll keep doing what I can
of what I was doing before.
Staying safe and sane
now my only goal.

Yes, I'll learn to color my own hair.
Give myself something that resembles a pedicure.
And yes, it's not lost on me that reaching my toes
would be so much easier with a beach body.

The real question now is
"what is worth dying for?"

I'll pull my circle inward.
Air hug my grands masked

And hope against all hope
that it's all enough.

ABOUT THIS POEM

A phenomenon that grew almost immediately once "sheltering-in-place" began was overachieving online. Zoom classes and meetings popping up for your every need: church, exercise, art classes, and on and on. We were all stuck at home so why not do all those things you never had time for before? Be even more efficient; "Marie Kondo" your drawers and closets. Apparently, she has a folding method we all need to know. There was a groundswell of overachievers that picked up online where they left off in the real world. I, on the other hand, welcomed the break from routine, learned new ways to acquire the food I loved without leaving the couch, and decided staying safe and staying alive was now my main goal. My current pandemic body style closely resembles Russian Nesting Dolls and I'm okay with that.

MY RELIGION

Organizing my refrigerator is therapy.
Gathering like things into special bins,
cheeses, butters vegan and regular.
Stowing leftovers on the top shelf, at eye level,
to avoid losing sight of important things.

Sometimes I even take pictures.
Sending them to friends
I know will compliment my organizational skills,
or envy my household's commitment
to a vegan lifestyle.

The healthy food I make for my vegan husband is his love cup.
The stacking, the rows, the tidiness of a place for everything.
Goodness waiting to be released from airtight containers
lifts him up.

Together we spend a lot of time anticipating the next meal.
Mine usually tied to wants and whims.
His to top shelf delicacies of born-again deliciousness.

My Covid-19 companion, Boredom and I,
Spend most days remembering abundance and freedom.
Believing in a return to the Promised Land very soon.

POST COVID

There's a world outside my door after Covid-19.
But for now I'm enjoying my bed.
Sleep is but a dream, pun intended.
When I awaken, I linger.
I used to jump right up.
What was I thinking?
The world doesn't need to start like a foot race.

Now I lounge and do morning bed ballet.
I move into positions with my wedged pillow under my legs.
Toe pointed, head turned to the side, eyes casting upward.
Feeling completely supported.
Perhaps I'll move into bed yoga one day.

I'm a little chagrined that I bought into the bedroom sleeping sanctuary lore.
The idea that a television creates bad Feng Shui. "Eff that!"
Now, I shamelessly go to bed with Rachel Maddow many nights.
I also play my game Hue on my phone, comfortably pillowed up.
It's become like a second office or a third if you count my art room.

There's a world outside my door after Covid-19.
When I cross that finish line, my new lessons will come with me.
I'll breathe deeper, lay longer, live life in manageable bites.
I won't buy into current culture myths.
Who do they think they are anyway?

There's a world outside my door after Covid-19.
When I go there I'll be a better version of me.
Less influenced by the outside.
More connected to the inside.
More grateful, happy, and free.

OBITUARY FOR THE BRA

Brassiere - Nickname "Bra"
Born/Patented 1914
Went to be with its maker March 2020
Cause of death Covid-19 related
Preceded in death by the Corset
Survived by Bralette and Sports Bra

The Bra lived a long, industrious life, enhancing breast size, creating cleavage, and idealizing culturally preferred breast shapes. Truth be known, her popularity had been sagging for years. Bra manufacturers were careful to point out that bras only affect the shape of the breast while being worn (*Wikipedia*). This brought on a resounding "DUH" from anyone who has ever had a breast or seen one.

A big part of the Bra's job was to hide the scandalous nipples. You know, the ones we feed our babies with. Little known fact: The term "Hand Bra" refers to women using their hands to cover their nipples in a pornographic film. I don't know how my husband knew that!

Once the coronavirus pandemic got into full swing and stay-at-home orders were issued, women everywhere began rising up asking "why are we wearing these uncomfortable contraptions?" Maybe it was because they realized they could die at any minute or maybe because every woman knows the best part of her day is when she gets home and takes her bra off.

It didn't really matter why. One-by-one, women started freeing themselves, shedding the undergarments that had been thrust upon them since puberty.

A celebration of life would be poorly attended. So with no further adieu, we bid farewell to brassieres everywhere. May they rest in peace in the back of the lingerie drawer, where they can't hurt anyone anymore.

In lieu of flowers, please social distance, and for God's sake, wear a fucking mask.

YOU CAN HAVE

Today you can have the cool mist of the rain that just fell.
The wave that lapped on shore as the boat passed.
You can have the thunder that boldly announces itself "BOOM!"

You can have the joy of more days on the planet
And the tears that come from your mother far away.
Her memory moving even farther away.

You can have judgment about how you spend your Covid-19 days.
You can have terror about what we are still learning.
Anxiety about not knowing how long this beast of an uninvited
guest will stay.

You can have knowing that you are living history.
Which we always knew.
Except now it takes on a foreboding quality.

You can have rainbows and parades in your mind.
You can have memories of togetherness
That now might threaten your survival.

You can wax nostalgic
For your concert days and Jumbotrons.
Your TV is your Jumbotron now.

The thunder claps "BOOM!"

Announcing the boats have been burned.
No going back.

Like it or not, a new way is born.

NIGHTMARE ON COVID STREET

It's not when the second story bathtub overflowed.
And I try to carry a leaky pillow case full of milk.
Not the waking up from a blackout driving.
Not the terror trying to drive from the backseat.
Not the confusion arriving at the hospital.
Not the not knowing where to go.
Not all the unmasked people passing me.
Not my panic as I reach up realizing I'm not masked.
Not me frantically searching for the one I always carry.
Not the hospital employee saying "They do things differently here"
And me wondering "Is different good?
Not the dark haired, big eyed woman who seems to know me.
Who sits too close as I continue looking for my mask.
Who empties her purse, some of her things touching mine.
"I don't have a business card" she finally says.
"That's okay" I say. "I'll be dead soon anyway."
It's not when she leans in and asks "what's your diagnosis?"
Not my closed throat response.
"I don't have one but some really weird shit has been happening."
Not even then.

It's when she looks deeply into my eyes.
And slowly nods her head and I nod mine.

That's when I become completely undone.

*Inspired by "What Belongs to Us" by Marie Howez

ABOUT THIS POEM

After shelter-in-place orders were issued, Covid-19 invaded all aspects of our days and nights. It was like elevator music playing in the background of everything. Soon it invaded my dreams, too. Almost a year later, masks and Covid-19 make their way into my dreams regularly. I'm a vivid dreamer as you can probably tell by this edited version of a nightmare I had early on in the pandemic.

AFTER THE PAUSE

I may weep in grocery stores.
My heart may ache forever
for the sacrifices of the world.

I may see my grandparent's life
in a whole new light.

The family table, with stored leaves
holding childhood memories,
may not get passed on.

Because of the pause,
I miss my father more.
I have his blue eyes to keep me company.
Not in a jar; that would be weird.

He wasn't much of a talker
but he knew things.
I long for certainty,
for people who know things.

My grand darling said to me
"I like your YouTube Channel."
For her, I'm the one with blue eyes
who knows things.

TEN OOPS ELEVEN THINGS ABOUT COVID-19

1. Sometimes I'm not sure what day it is and I rather like it. Today feels like a Sunday although it's a Tuesday. I know people out in the world need to know what day it is but I don't.

2. I miss some people and not others. I don't always miss my obligation people. I love them dearly but the intersection between want and "need to" gets tricky.

3. I have a hard time calling my mom on a regular basis. With a compromised memory, our conversations are pretty much always the same. How's the weather, etc. My counselor tells me "all the same" can be comforting to someone with memory issues. I'm trying that on for size.

4. My son and grands are the only people I see. Masked, socially distanced, mostly outside. I love seeing them but I have some worry and regret after. Some fear of "what if?"

5. It got colder here today and good news, my jeans fit. Hoping not to have a second wave of weight gain in the second wave of Covid-19 or is this the third wave?

6. I shop nearly 100% online. It's weird and comforting at the same time. I feel enormously lucky I can buy what I want and need.

7. Soon it will be longer than a year since I have traveled. That part feels weird. I was always a plane ride away from anyone or anything or so I thought. Now the miles stretch farther.

8. I never imagined something like this. Wouldn't have believed it. And now here we are 10 months in. By now it feels like time has passed quickly, earlier not so much,

9. I will be one of the first in line for the vaccine. It's funny thinking about that line, being in it feels a bit like a dream right now.

10. I haven't yet lost any of "my people" but so many have, young and old. When I hear about people who treated Covid-19 like a hoax getting it, I smile a little smile, not a happy one, a "see it's not a hoax" one. They still somehow manage to downplay it. That's a whole 'nother skill set.

11. Trump for me will always be associated with Covid-19. He didn't cause it but he sure fucked up the response to it. Teflon Don, not his fault cause nothing sticks to him.

CHAINSAW DAY

Monday, a tree fell across our driveway in a storm, a BIG tree, probably 15 feet high where it snapped off. Twenty feet of it is now laying on the ground in the "foresty" area crossing the path of our gravel driveway, A BIG TREE, fifteen inches in diameter.

Luckily, Bob's baby chainsaw was man enough for the parts blocking the driveway. The rest will remain in perpetuity on our forest floor because it is way too big for us to move and it looks at home there.

It reminded me of the hundreds of thousands of trees snapped off like broken matchsticks in Hurricane Michael.

We didn't even see the downed tree until the following morning when we were leash walking the cat, yeah we leash walk our cat. Don't you?

After the WOW, my only thought was clearing the driveway. I joked on Facebook about how I get a lot of packages delivered these days.

"Glad you are okay" most friends commented. It never occurred to me to worry or be upset let alone not be okay. My only thought was clearing the driveway before heat exhaustion set in. It's Florida, not a dry heat here.

It was only in the late afternoon, after a ton of well-wishers were glad I was okay (probably impressed by the photos) did it occur to me that the tree could have fallen on me and I wouldn't have been okay.

This is how Bob and I operate in the pandemic. We get up, do one "big job on our list" only one, and then fill the day with other things we want or need to do. Believe it or not, that day was already designated "chainsaw day." We had a low, head banger branch, on the big oak tree out back. Our work got slightly expanded.

Right now, I don't fear much past the coronavirus. It's almost the only thing that heightens my awareness. Not getting it is job one; all the other stuff is noise. Getting up, putting one foot in front of the other, going to bed, and doing it all again the next day always mindful of all the precautions to stay safe.

Today, I read a woman's writing on Facebook about her experience having Covid-19. I felt so much empathy for her and what she went through. She wrote about how one of her non-mask wearing friends responded with a condescending "sweetie" like it couldn't have been that bad. The woman said she felt like cutting her off. I stopped reading at "cutting her."

THE STRAW

I used to be the strong one.
Now I feel like a puddle on the floor needing to be wiped up.
Like a broken toy, broken glass, a broken heart,
Broken person, friend, daughter, Mimi, wife, shopper,
caregiver, warrior princess.
My hope has been hijacked.

Why do we remember the straw that broke the camel's back
and not the thousands of straws that came before it?
Yesterday, a squirrel scurried by carrying a big pine cone.
Too big, I believed, for him to scale the eight foot fence.
Initially, I was right. He barely made it half way up before falling
back.
But then he doubled his efforts sailing over the fence, pine cone
and all.

I need a small win. A tiny grace will do.
One that registers an upward tic at the corner of my mouth.
One that tells me this six month wall I'm slamming into
won't break me.

It could be as small as finding my phone the first place I look.
Or getting a good night's sleep or a dream where I fly.
A small thing right now,
could feel like a fucking miracle.

BLIND FAITH

As the fog thickens, we accelerate.
No way to know how fast we are going.
We can't see the things we are whizzing by.
We fool ourselves thinking boundaries are safe.
A massive pile up may be in our future.
And still, we continue moving forward.

Sam taught me how I greet people.
He says "Mimi, are you good?"
Echoing my words when I see him.
Perhaps I should ask "how are you doing?"
But the truth is I want you to be good.
So I steer you where I want you to go.

I also want to enjoy daily exercise.
To see friends I miss and others I don't.
For loved ones near and far to remain safe.
For life to lift everyone up not just a few.
And for hope and help and happiness to rule.

TRANQUIL

Have you been surprised how fast and slow it all feels?
How holding two contradictory thoughts at once
seems a hallmark of the pandemic.
How it doesn't even feel weird anymore.
How comfortable the solitude has become.
How mixing it up can be
as simple as making a fancy aioli for your homemade beet burger.

How time and space and cleaning the house
have fallen into new categories
like maybe tomorrow,
or sometime next week,
or why bother, no one's coming over.

How you can get up in the middle of the night
because a poem begs to be written.
How it's not a big deal if you're tired tomorrow.
You're retired. It was never a big deal but you sure made it one.
How you follow your muse around more letting her run things.

How the garage door spring breaking with the car inside
doesn't even faze you. You weren't going anywhere anyway.
How "old you" tries to make a big deal out of it
saying "what if there's an emergency?"
and still it doesn't gain traction.

How time stands still,
so still you imagine you are the only one in the world.
Then you hear a car driving down the road
and you know you're not alone
because someone is driving that car.

How apocalyptic it all feels
and yet you can't seem to spell apocalyptic.
So you scribble it a little lest someone sees it
and realizes you are not perfect.
What a relief that would be.

How sometimes, too many times,
you get halfway through the writing
and can't recall where you were going
or what you are even thinking
and how utterly okay that all is.

I've been surprised how accepting I can be of the restrictions.
How much peace there is in just saying, admitting,
"I can't. It doesn't feel right for me."
AND how many times in my life
I said that very same thing…and then did it anyway.

How good it feels to listen,
to finally get so quiet
I have no choice
but to listen to myself,
uninterrupted by the rest of the world.

THE COUCH

We only got a new couch once when I was growing up.
Mom was proud to create this unique space in our tiny house,
identical to all the others in our neighborhood.
I believe it was a brown sectional, tucked tightly into the corner,
perfectly making the ninety degree turn towards the front door.

I could check the Super 8 home movies to verify.
But that would make me seem super old so I won't.
We were told "don't put your feet on the couch,
don't play on the couch, sit up straight on the couch."
Our old furniture asked so much less of us.

I'm not sure where they purchased it.
I don't think with the Green Stamps the grocery store gave out.
We licked them, put them into books, saved them,
and counted the books, until we had enough for a desired item.
We did get our card table and four chairs with Green Stamps.

I was always fascinated by Freud and analysis.
The pictures of patients lying on couches
with an analyst behind them taking copious notes.
The couch was considered clinical yet intimate enough for the process.
One rule "the patient must say anything that comes into their mind."
I thought that would be really fun since most of the time,

I was told to be quiet and keep things to myself.

I got married at eighteen.
I didn't have to. I just needed to get out of the house.
I ended up in therapy.
Sitting, not lying, on a couch.
I was determined to unravel the mystery of me.
Determined not to let the rest of my life be
an apology for my first big decision.
Determined to find the courage
to create the future I so desperately wanted.

Bob and I got married when Matt was four.
We waited until Matt was in fourth grade to buy new furniture.
We could have afforded it sooner,
but I didn't want to be the mom saying "don't play on the couch."
Instead, I was the mom a little bit obsessed with spills.
Matt had to use sippy cups well into middle school.
On sleepovers, his friends thought it was fun.
Add the crazy slippers "Santa" brought every year
and you had a theme party.

In these Covid-19 times, I'm in therapy, again.
I have a tele-therapist. She's quite amazing.
I even read my poetry to her.
She helps me navigate the ups and downs.
It was a rough couple of years before the pandemic.
2020 was supposed to be my celebration year.
Instead, I find myself dialing into an online health portal.

As I wait for my therapist to join the call,
I notice there's a room scene on the screen.

It has a couch icon.

How perfect is that!

REVEALING

A poem doesn't care it's Thanksgiving.
That coronavirus is killing us.
Doesn't care about social distancing.
Or your clever plan to use tray tables.
Or that you will bring your own serving spoons.

It cares about a different kind of space.
Spaces you ignore, corners you avoid.
The poem wants you to look under things.
It wants you to feel the rhythm and beat.
It wants you to dance in new worlds.

The poem demands a lot to be sure.
It tries to grab you by your "Unawares."
Shaking you to see what's in your pockets.
Some will close the book or find a new page.
The poem is okay with what happens.

The poem remembers a simpler time.
Finding contrast with harder ones, too.
It dreams of a world fully united.
It hopes for freedom and understanding.
Hopes our delicate democracy lives.

A poem eats and breathes and sleeps.
Yells and screams and hugs and loves.

A poem rebels, resists, and persists.
Sometimes it surprises you.
Or do you surprise yourself?

UNTIL NOW

In the past two years Pre-Covid-19, life has been pitching me fastballs and curveballs but hasn't managed to strike me out. I didn't hit all home runs but I got on base every time my number was called. Believe me, in those two years it was called way too often. When needed, I even made a "circus catch" or two.

Elton John's song "*Still Standing*" best captures how I feel right now. "…I'm still standing better than I ever did. Looking like a true survivor, feeling like a little kid." I can't really explain it. Maybe for the last two years, I was in training for all of this. Perhaps we all have been training all our lives for the spot we stand in today.

My biggest fear isn't Covid-19. I'll do my best, wash my hands, mask up, and stay in place until I truly believe I can re-enter the world safely. My biggest fear is the lack of effective leadership and our failure as a country.

My worst nightmare is a world where we continue to pretend that up is down and down is up. It's not possible for me to drink enough to make that okay for four more years. Please God, don't make me prove that wrong.

Our survival hinges on humanity, compassion, fairness, rule of law, all things we took for granted until now. We won't go back to Pre-Covid-19 times just like we won't go back to Pre-Trump times. Our best hope is to hit a grand slam in the 2020 election and install a new president.

Then we can take the lessons learned and create a future where we slow down and appreciate the little things. Where people come first and money comes second. Where we are "true survivors" and can still feel the joy of being a little kid.

PART 3

Personal Hurricanes

WEREN'T WE BEAUTIFUL

Weren't we beautiful,
The way I stood on the first step to hug you, heart to heart.
You so tall my heart always felt like it was reaching for yours.

We thought we had all the time in the world.
In many ways we still do, even now,
Even after all that's happened.

We are so beautiful together
Even unshowered, even in fits of anger,
Even when no one is watching.

What an unlikely thing us together.
Our differences didn't outweigh our love.
Isn't that just the most beautiful thing.

ALL IN

Let's say the story goes like this.
Boy meets girl, they marry and live happily ever after.
But a lot happens in that happily ever after.

If they're lucky, and I do mean frightfully lucky,
They will get an ever after,
And sometimes a happy one.

Being married is hard.
Forty years,
Jesus that's a forever.

And then a big challenge comes, and he could die,
Leave her all alone.
Well that doesn't sound right or fair or or or....

Then the winds blow
In the most beautiful of directions.
They get a second chance.

She was always "all in."
But now she knows
What "all in" really is.

BEFORE

Before Hurricane Michael on October 10, 2018
Before Bob's mother's brain tumor diagnosis two days before Hurricane Michael
Before Bob's own tongue and tonsil cancer diagnosis two days after her death
Before Bob's unsuccessful robotic surgery at the Mayo Clinic two days after her funeral
Before a second unrelated rare primary tumor was discovered on the PET scan
Before Bob's 6 ½ weeks of radiation at MD Anderson in Houston
Before Bob's abdominal surgery for the second primary tumor

We had our future planned.
With luck and good decisions, we created a financially secure life.
Bob took early retirement.
We moved to Panama City Beach to be close to our son and grands.
We pedaled hard together all those years.
Now we were looking forward to the downhill part.
Then came Cancer.

I STOPPED WRITING

Maybe I thought if there was no record of it, it wouldn't be true.
Maybe I didn't know what to say.
All I knew was the thing that took my breath away
stole my pen, too.

I hadn't written a word
since I heard my husband loudly say,
"Fuck, Fuck, Fuck, I have Cancer."

It had been a shitty year.
Son's divorce, Cat 5 Hurricane, Bob's mother's brain tumor and subsequent death.
Now this, I pleaded, please not this.
A shit sandwich we never ordered but would have to eat.

"What are you talking about? You do not!" I said.
The computer screen lit his troubled face as he read the CT scan report.
He loaded the disk needing to see the tumor with his own eyes and I cried reading "Malignant until proven otherwise" in all caps.

BEAM ME UP

I say "we have cancer" because what happens to one of us happens to both of us. When Bob was first diagnosed, I couldn't write. Writing made it feel too real. Slowly, I found my voice again and began writing each day for 6 ½ weeks as I waited for Bob to finish his daily Proton Beam Radiation treatment.

Day 1 - I keep staring at the door waiting for it to open, waiting for him to return to tell me how he is, what it was like, hoping to hear words like "okay" or "no big deal," not wanting to hear anything else.

Waiting is my new job. I call all the support people in the room "The Waiters." It's the kids that grab my heart and won't let go. Hair missing, some so sick they are rolled out of the same door my eyes return to every time it opens and shuts. Young kids covered with their blankets from home with cartoon characters on them, lying motionless, as they are wheeled onto the elevator. Bob finally walks through the door I've been staring at all this time. "How was it?" I ask. "Tolerable" he says and now we have begun.

Our 33 days go much like this. Usually involving hours of waiting and a cast of characters that I get to know well. As time progresses, we see patients with large bandages, red faces and necks. Those further along in their treatment than us who someday we know we will be. Every day, I choose the chair that offers the best view of the door while I wait.

I look up each time the door opens even though I know it's too soon. I feel an affinity to those waiting here with me. They live, like me in the space within two feet of their bodies. I recognize this in myself and others. It was the only space I felt like I had control of when we were first diagnosed. It was the only place I could find peace.

I woke up weepy this morning. Weepy has become a part of my process. For five to ten minutes a day I let what's happening wash over me. It's my release valve for the mounting pressure. I hear a noise and turn toward the door. Nope, not him yet. I wonder if this feeling will ever end. By the end, will I not even notice the opening and closing of the door? Will I look up and just see him standing in front of me by the table where I sit each day? I hear a loud waterfall in the waiting room that I never noticed before. Perhaps my mind just got quiet enough to notice.

Today all the people in the waiting room seem like fresh faces. That's what happens as time goes by. More and more people finish their treatment, ring the Gong, and new ones start. I did learn the noisy night receptionist guy's name is Devin. He's quite funny and engaging and always loud in the process. For me, the people working here are the supporting cast in this daily one act play called "Bob's Radiation."

Out of the corner of my eye, I see a mom, dad, and child with a full head of sandy colored hair walk down the spiral staircase. They seem immune to the disarming charm of Devin's rowdy hello. The mom carries her son's green mask, a smaller version of Bob's. I still remember the first day when Bob carried his in. She sits down and lets the comfy chair support her all too heavy head for a moment before moving back to the table to set up markers and an activity book for her son. Dad gets a soda and disappears. When he walks back down the spiral staircase the boy gives his father the sweetest wave and dad waves back. The tension between the couple could be cut with a knife. In a few minutes, the door opens and a name is called. The young mother rises and disappears through the door that I always watch, taking with her the mask that is apparently hers. The dad and curly haired boy stay seated. They are her "Waiters" now. I fight back tears and lose.

Only a few days left. I follow Bob down the all too familiar spiral staircase. He checks in and I head for the couch. Lonnie, a Texan we've gotten to know, is here. Bob waves to him. He looks different. When he makes a slow walk to the desk using a cane, I realize he's not wearing his signature cowboy hat. I overhear Lonnie say he can't eat much because the sores from the radiation are driving him crazy. I look over a few minutes later and a man sitting next to Lonnie asks if he minds if he says a prayer for him. The two men join a single hand. The man takes off his baseball cap and Lonnie lowers his head and the prayer commences. I overhear the man thanking God for meeting Lonnie today and think to myself "that is just the best prayer ever."

Finally, our last day arrives. All the regulars seem to be in the waiting room. Lonnie tells us he's hanging in there. Bob goes back for his last radiation treatment. Now I'm watching the door for a different reason. When the door opens, they call my name to come back with him.

It’s time to ring the gong!

Woohoo!

Ding Dang Done!

POST-OP NURSE GETS A MESSAGE

We kiss goodbye. I turn and walk away without looking back.
Just like I did when we moved to California.
Just like I always do.

The nurse points me down a long hallway where I'll wait.
I pick a spot and settle in for my 6- 8 hour day.
The staff hasn't arrived just yet.

At 8 am, a volunteer circles the room with a clipboard,
jotting down names, phone numbers, and locations
for regularly scheduled updates.

10 am Update:
Bubbly clipboard lady leads me to a private room.
A nurse enters and begins speaking in a rote manner.
"Procedure began at 7:52 am.
Your husband is tolerating the surgery well.
A definitive decision on the Whipple has not been made."
And as quickly as she arrived, she is gone.

Bubbly clipboard lady tells me my next update will be at noon.
The seat I had been sitting in is now occupied.
No problem, I take an open seat nearby.

An entire extended family of twenty has taken up residence.
Bob's brother Jack arrives to wait with me.

We laugh at this huge gathering wondering who could possibly be left at home.

A big noisy family, uncles high fiving 4 year olds, and everyone talking loud.
We decide to give them their own space and move to a different area.
I walk to the desk to tell clipboard lady my new location.

Before I say anything she says "Albers? Dr. Katz is ready to talk to you."
"But it's not noon yet!" I say.
I run back to get Jack and head to the update room.

My mind races "is this good news or bad news?"
For the past six months, every single time we saw Doctor Katz,
I asked about the chances of removing only the tumor.

Every single time he told me "minuscule"
and looked at me like "you know what minuscule means, right?"
Unfortunately, I did.

Dr. Katz walks in and tells us something not minuscule at all.
He removed the tumor with 1 millimeter to spare.
The Whipple was not needed.

I'm the giddy and bubbly one now.
I thank him for being so good at what he does.
Because he is obviously the best at what he does.

Back in the waiting area, I feel this euphoric shock.
I keep shaking my head, so relieved, so grateful,
wanting this moment to never end.

In The Recovery Room:
Bob is a little groggy, but awake.
Duane, his post-op nurse tells us "when I receive a message
'Patient didn't get the planned surgery'
It's not usually good news."
Today, it was incredibly good news.
That the three of us celebrated together!

I have a picture of the night sky, in Houston, Texas.
On surgery day, August 19, 2019.
The happiest day of my life.

GRATEFUK

I invented a new word. I was trying to type grateful but something went haywire.

As Bob recovers at home, we are grateful for so many things, the biggest one our miracle that the tumor could be completely removed without him needing a life-changing Whipple procedure. He only lost a gallbladder and a rare tumor and we can live quite nicely with that.

But when your world gets turned upside down, it isn't over for a very long time. Maybe in some ways, it's never over. I can't know that just yet. There are so many things I am grateful beyond measure for and a few that I am a little gratefuk about.

Bob plays ukulele and sings. We had band practice at our house on Sunday. It's always so much fun. It's like a big family. They play for a while then we share a big spread of food (old normal). Bob will play his first gig on Thursday. For a few more weeks, he will probably need a stool when he would normally stand but that feels like nothing now.

Bob is kinda obsessed with his scar, like me and my hair. He sent a picture to the surgeon to make sure it was healing correctly. It's a long scar and different parts of it are healing at different rates, all very normal.

I do want my "old normal" back. Please don't mention "a new normal" because I might jump on you. Old normal is returning slowly. That's how healing happens, s-l-o-w-l-y! I'm not good at slowly or "a new normal" but I'm getting better. At least, I can say it without clenching my teeth and growling now. Gratefuk for that!

CHRISTMAS EVE 2019

Well grief, you did visit me but not in the way I expected.

At the end of a truly wonderful Christmas Eve, Bob headed up to bed. In the twinkling of the tree lights, the weight of the last year hit me. I expected it on the first anniversary of his mom's death in early December or the anniversary of his first surgery a few days before Christmas, but nothing came until now.

Through tears, I cradled Tux apologizing for not being the cat mom he deserved all last year. The memories flooded in. Last Christmas Eve, a few days out of surgery, Bob ran out of pain medication. His doctors were five hours away at Mayo in Jacksonville and the prescription could not be called in, so they mailed it. Thanks "War on Drugs!" Cancer patients are not the drug addicts you're looking for.

In the meantime, I started thinking about which of my friends had a recent surgery or root canal that I might "borrow" some medication from to get us by until the prescription came. I used my "phone a friend lifeline" and scored some pain pills to help with the enormous amount of pain he was in.

With each dose, Bob spent the hour before his next scheduled pain pill in agony holding frozen water bottles kept in a cooler beside the bed to his jaw line for some relief. I passed the hours rubbing his hands and feet trying to relax him. I felt utter helplessness seeing him in so much pain.

That was the beginning of our year long march to healing, robotic surgery, healing, radiation, healing, second tumor surgery, healing.

Tears cried tonight were sad tears for what we've been through and happy ones, too, for where we are now…grateful and no longer feeling helpless.

BAD HAIR DAY

Well, nothing says Happy New Year like jury duty on January 3rd. I got excused last summer when Bob was in cancer treatment. People are super sweet to you when your husband has cancer. Back then, January seemed so far off. Now, my calendar is full of lots of important things, like dog sitting for Rosie our grand puppy (a phrase I thought I'd never utter). Rosie belongs to my son and his girlfriend. My son didn't want a dog. A girlfriend wasn't on his radar either until his marriage of twelve years and two kids suffered a surprise divorce. She's mostly housebroken, the puppy, not the girlfriend.

I can't help but worry about going to jury duty and leaving Rosie alone with Bob. I'm not sure he has the skill set for it. It takes noticing and predicting. She's a puppy and needs reminding to "go pee." A bigger problem is the bald eagle that has taken up residence in the tall, dead pine left behind by Hurricane Michael. All my friends say "bald eagle sightings are blessings." I can't agree this time. I follow Rosie around the yard like a hawk. The whole time I fantasize about the bird swooping down and having to punch a bald eagle the size of a first grader in the face, which is probably illegal, and definitely ill-advised. But that's what grandparents do!

I consider trying to get out of jury duty but pet sitting doesn't appear on the list of acceptable excuses. On jury day, I get up early to review the dress code. A couple of years ago when my husband served, they sent him home to change clothes. That's not happening to me. I decide on gray slacks, a bright turquoise blouse, a tie-dyed scarf (a nod to my politics), and my thick, black glasses that make me look super smart. I notice one side of my hair has a mind of its own but I don't have time to fool with it.

The jury summons warns me to arrive a half hour early because there is limited parking. On the "Comment Card" I'll suggest they get more parking. I arrive at the courthouse and join a long line for the metal detector that snakes out the door and down the sidewalk. I'm cursed with a friendly face and the woman in front of me strikes up a conversation more like a rant. I learn she isn't here for jury duty. She's here to pay a $500 fine because her dog keeps getting out and her "asshole neighbor" keeps turning her in. She's late for work and not happy.

When I reach the front of the line, I put my purse and jacket on the metal detector's conveyor belt. The officer sets a bowl down, gestures toward my wrist and instructs me to remove my Fitbit. "My Fitbit, really" I say.

Once inside, the Clerk of Courts welcomes us and begins rattling on about our jury system being the best in the world. I think he's trying to make us feel better about being there but it's not working.

Over a hundred of us are seated in wooden church-like pews. On the back of the pew in front of me someone roughly scratched "fuck" into the wood. I nod in agreement. Further down someone named Blake also left a scratched autograph. Sidebar Blake: So many questions. Did you know your name is not ordinary? Did you think there might be cameras in here? What did you get through the metal detector to accomplish this feat?

The waiting is over; now it's down to business. We're told about the cases needing juries this week and how long they are expected to last. One is a criminal trial expecting to last one day. I immediately set my sights on that one. I start imagining myself watching grainy surveillance video and saying "yes the defendant is that burglar."

I secretly "thumbs up" myself when my number is called for questioning by the judge and lawyers for the criminal trial. We all answer from the same list of questions. "Have you or anyone in your immediate family ever been charged with a felony?" If the answer was "yes" they asked "Did you feel like you were treated well by the justice system." I don't know where they found all these people but they all said they were treated well. The final question "Can you be impartial?" I wonder if they mean "Mitch McConnell impartial" or regular impartial but I decide not to ask and simply say "YES."

With the jury pool questioning complete, the judge reads the charges. "Sexual Battery" involving a twelve year old child and a couple of other charges, but I can't hear anything over the noise of a freight train screeching to a halt in my mind.

I'm not a gambler, but I keep reminding myself there are twenty-one potential jurors in this box. Only seven will be chosen. Those are pretty good odds.

My mind starts racing. "Did they like me too much?" This happens. "Was I too approachable? Did I make too much eye contact? Did I look at the defendant?" I know I did. "Did I seem sympathetic to the prosecutor when she pointed out the defendant's lawyer blatantly misrepresented her statement?" I should have tried harder not to. "Will my friendly face bite me on the ass? Should I have chosen to wear my peace sign earrings today?"

Now we wait while the judge, attorneys, and defendant all sidebar together to pick six jurors and one alternate. In Florida, six jurors are standard unless the case involves the death penalty. As we wait, the woman seated next to me decides to confess she is not sure she can be impartial. Now I'm met with the moral dilemma "do I narc on her?"

When the names of the jurors chosen are read, the woman next to me remains seated and I join the small line of seven that none of us wants to be in. I give my contact information and cell phone number to the clerk.

I can't help but wonder, if I had taken the time to fix the bad side of my hair this morning, would things have gone differently.

WHILE I WAIT

I wonder how we remain standing
when life seems to take so much from us
ask so much of us.

I wonder how people with Cancer keep showing up
expecting this will be the treatment,
protocol, snake oil to cure them.

I wonder if they think about life without us
like we do them
or do they just think about life without life.

I wonder about people who say
"I hope this mess is over soon."
I don't think they understand pandemics.

He's seeing the doctor now for a checkup.
Patients only for everyone's safety.
I wonder what the doctor is saying.

I wonder why people who seem to do everything right
don't always get right outcomes.
I wonder what the doctor is saying.

I wonder if I became ill would he be a great caregiver.
I doubt it. We are who we are.

The sooner we all realize that the better.

I wonder if I'll pop open the bubbly
before noon today because
it's good news or bad news.

I wonder if he will be reassured
or if he'll get a heavy bag of uncertainty
to haul home and carry.

I wonder what the doctor is saying.
No text yet....

Wait, Wait...he just texted.

"I'M OKAY! HAPPY DANCE!"

Happy dance indeed!

I love what the doctor said!

A SWEET SURPRISE

After years of me asking "what are you thinking" to engage him in conversation, he now talks at length, about the blackberries, the garden, the yard, and the state of our world.

He tells me about the blackberries, how last year we didn't mow down that little area between the fence and the lagoon, about how it takes two years to get blackberries, the first year the blossoms and the second the fruit. But that's not where the story begins.

He tells me about the wispy wasp. The one that has a delicate nest, paper-like not honeycomb. He thinks the wasps eat the fruit too. He says there's plenty for everyone. Having fruit grow in your yard is quite exciting during a pandemic but that's not where the story begins.

A slow pace suits him. Picking blackberries suits him. Leisurely walks with the cat on leash suits him. Watching YouTube videos suits him. Spending hours and hours puzzling puzzles suits him.

Yesterday, he told me that it may be close to the end of blackberry season. I got all teary eyed. I'll miss his berry picking jaunts and his proud smile as he shows me his bounty. I'll miss the cobblers, too, but that's not where the story begins.

The story begins with Bob being mowed down last year by two surgeries for two cancers and one dreadful 6 ½ week radiation stint and the care and energy it took to come back from that.

It's hard to explain how a year can feel long and short at the same time. How my heart broke seeing him in pain. How the future we'd hoped for took an uncertain turn and still we got up every day and walked toward it together.

We had no idea our limited energy for yard work and not mowing beyond the fence was creating a sweet, well-timed, surprise, the blackberries. We didn't know how much conversation and joy those little berries could bring us while we self-isolated for Covid-19. Some things you just never know until you do.

PART 4

Pathways

NAMING

At birth they called me Caren Sue Browning.
A breach baby, one toe over the line.
Struggled living in a house of conflict.
Trying to find out what love really was.

Found a way out. Got married at eighteen.
To a kind and boring man who loved me.
My name is Caren Sue Browning Rieser.
A beautiful son. A friendly divorce.

Love at first sight? Laughing, I saw his soul.
A touch conveyed love. A word conveyed love.
Everything I'd longed for and so much more.
I'm Caren Sue Browning Rieser Albers.

Spent my middle decades learning, healing.
With two steps forward, then one step backward.
Even then, you eventually get there.
Friends, lots of them, call me Caren Albers.

One friend, attempting to hurt me, said
"I didn't know you were capable of that!"
Her attempt at manipulation empowered me.
No she didn't.

Letting go of stories about lacking.

Gaining confidence in myself, my life.
Moving forward joyfully, happily.
I become an artist and a writer.

I write my first book, *Happiness Junkie.*
Twelve steps to find inner peace and change your life.
Next *Married to a Vegan* 'cause I was.
Humor, food, and happy relationships.

My love mate of forty years gets cancer.
My clarity ninja skills kick in.
The best treatment, latest technology.
Surgery, radiation, surgery.

I learn to spell Paraganglioma.
Foot soldiers finding our way together.
Each day, one foot in front of the other.
Walking to "no evidence of disease."

I'm Caren Sue Browning Rieser Albers.
My life is full and healthy and happy.
I stand up for truth and fairness and love.
My true friends never underestimate me.

STAYING AFLOAT

I spent half my life trying
to keep my head above water:
feet scissor kicking, treading, hands madly forming figure eights.
If that failed, I pretended to swim
but really I dog paddled.

When exhaustion came,
(and exhaustion always came)
I rolled over, defeated, and
floated on my back.
The whole time hoping for
someone to rescue me,
to throw me a life preserver,
to jump in and pull me to safety...
But no one came.

It took fifty years and an ocean of tears
to learn how to save myself,
to learn that the CPR I needed
had to come from me,
to learn to fill my well of self love first,
to truly live, I must truly forgive,
that making everything look easy
keeps people from seeing the real me,
that healing comes in its own time,
that I am loved JUST AS I AM.

Staying afloat comes with greater ease now.
My buoyancy keeps me on top of the seas.
When I roll over, it's only to see
the stars twinkling triumphantly for me.

ABOUT THIS POEM

This poem began as five inches of water rose up against our house. As often happens in the Panhandle of Florida, too much rain comes way too quickly. I stood at the side door watching it rise, wishing it away, wondering when it would stop, and realizing like so many other things in life, I had no control over it. I started writing about my feeling powerless which led me to this heart song of acceptance and learning.

HOPING FOREVER

He was born a mountain stream, a youthful river. How long does the river remember?

Seems like only yesterday he said "I love you this much" stretching his arms as wide as they would go.
Only yesterday he giggled uncontrollably when she adorned his cheek with butterfly kisses.
Only yesterday she cheered for him at Little League games.
Only yesterday she taught him to drive a car.
He's been driving away ever since.

Her job was to teach him about life.
To manage, but not alter his flow.
To harness his energy and allow his tributaries their own path.
And hardest one of all, trust his choices.

She was good at her job, maybe too good.
He grew, thrived, loved, learned, and left.
Now she watches the river from a hilltop close by.
Admiring its strength and beauty.
In awe of its magnificent flow.

How long does the river remember?
She's hoping,
like the headwaters,
forever.

TOO MUCH TO ASK

From the road a beautiful house

In a nice neighborhood

Remodeled, it felt new

Spacious, no clutter

Essentials, nothing extra

Pantry stocked with Pop Tarts and Captain Crunch

Three stools lined the breakfast bar

A boy's room with superheroes

A girl's painted pink

He insisted their bedrooms be perfect

A large, inviting family room, purpose undiscovered

He needed a fresh start

He worried about their broken world

He hoped the beautiful pool out back

Would distract them

But that might be too much to ask

Even of a swimming pool

ABOUT THIS POEM

This poem grew out of helping my son put his life back together after an unexpected divorce. My heart broke for him and my two grandchildren. His youngest was the same age as he was when his father and I ended our marriage. I grieved again the ending of my own marriage and worried about the changes to come for all of them as I helped create their new world.

THE GIFT

Just before my first grand was born, friends raved about the wonders ahead of me.
They oohed and aahed and gushed telling me "it's a love like no other."
I listened earnestly, respectfully, and secretly thought "get a life people."
We were living in California far from family but visiting them often.

We were content and happy and planned more years there. Then came Sophia.
And oh how right they all were, times ten, maybe a hundred. We were smitten!
The first visit after she was born we started searching for a second home there.
"There" was the beautiful Emerald Coast, the panhandle of Florida.

The first year we visited once a quarter, loving the bond that was developing.
The second every two months by the third year we packed up and moved there.
It wasn't lost on me how wrong I was. Loving a grandchild is its own special animal.
We don't have to raise them; our only job is to love them. How perfect is that?

In one of my writing groups, our leader reads a poem and offers a jump-off line to write from.
We write for fifteen minutes, as poorly as possible, pen never leaving the paper.
It's stream of consciousness, letting go, getting into the flow, seeing what happens.
She offers this freeing statement to us "You don't have to do anything. We already love you."

That is the closest description I have to loving my two grandchildren.
An unconditional love that I didn't necessarily feel as a child.
I grew up thinking that my worth was tied to my performance.
That love could be given and therefore also taken away.

I said to a friend "You don't have to do anything. We already love you."
I realized how much we all need to hear this, sit with it, believe it.
We don't need to bring something special to the party.
We are the something special by showing up with our unique gifts.

If you've known me very long you've probably heard me say
Being here for my grands feels like my life's purpose.
Maybe a special need will materialize that I can fulfill best.
Or maybe, just maybe, I needed them, to teach me, about unconditional love.

RULE OF THREES

No one tells you that you won't sleep the night your father dies.
Would you even believe them?

With two days left on our vacation in Costa Rica.
The hotel room phone rings. It's my mother crying.
She sobs "Daddy died."

The doctor told him to enjoy himself.
We knew his heart would give out sometime.
But sometime came way too soon.

Later, I would explain to my mom the "Rule of Threes" for giving bad news.
You lead with something general, add to it, THEN deliver the bad news.

But that's not how bad news gets told.
It shoots out of you like a cannon.

For now, I just listen. Listen to the sunrise story.
How daddy doesn't usually go with her on a morning walk,
But today, he got up and went.
How she stayed at the pool while he got the tire checked.
How when she went inside, she thought he was just asleep.

I remember the rain dripping steadily down the window all night long.
I remember Bob holding me, having food brought to our room.
I remember hearing a siren wind its way up the curvy mountain road.

The next day I learned what had happened.

A child swimming in the hotel pool.
Had gone underwater.
And drowned.

If someone tells you that you won't sleep the night your father dies,
believe them.

LAUGHTER MULTIPLIES

I remember big holiday dinners with my now long-departed aunts and uncles. All the leaves of the table completely expanded with two rows of chairs scattered to accommodate a second tier of revelers. As a young child, sometimes I got to play under the dinner table.

I remember the jokes and the laughter continuing long after the dishes were cleared. I also remember the mashed potatoes. I would take small dinner rolls, the kind that came in their own little tin pans and spread mashed potatoes on them making my version of a mashed potatoes sandwich.

Several holidays, I was sent to the car for fighting with my Aunt Shirley. She was more like a cousin, four days older than me, and never let me forget it. Imagine my mom and Grandma P. having a baby the same week, one way too young, and one way too old.

Time waits for no one, days turned into weeks, weeks to months, and months to years until grandma couldn't wrestle the energy to prepare huge family dinners. Mom eventually arrived at that same door that I'm now peering at from a bit of distance but still seeing it.

The table where we gathered all those years sits in my dining room. It may not be passed on to a fifth generation and that's okay. People want to find their own ways and make their own memories and it had a good run.

I'll never forget the laughter. Someone would do an impression of great Uncle Hewitt's laugh, which sounds like he is gasping for air, and we probably shouldn't be laughing, and still we all laughed hard.

My love affair with mashed potatoes lives on, as does my love of that table, with the stored leaves, holding the laughter and memories of my childhood.

FOURTH FLOOR BALCONY

"Baby" my mom says. She knows I hate being called Baby. I'm a grown-ass woman. She senses my bristling and switches to "dear." "Dear, you're lucky your plane's getting out. Looks like the tropical storm may head right toward us here in Panama City Beach. Your sister and I aren't sure where to go in your townhome if severe weather hits."

Before I can stop myself "Fourth floor balcony" rolls off my tongue. I picture gale force winds blowing her up, up, and away. Luckily, she laughs, and then I laugh, too. A better daughter would have just thought it, but my older sister snapped up the "good daughter" title and my younger sister is the baby of the family. Guess I'm destined to be the wise-cracking warrior.

This isn't the first time we've had this "best safe place" conversation. On a previous year, in another condo, as the tornado sirens blasted, my mother tried to convince me to seek shelter in the second story bathroom. I maintained that an interior space on the first floor offered the most protection. Neither of us would concede. So as she hunkered down in the upstairs bath, I retreated to the first floor closet yelling over the blare of sirens, "If the tornado hits, we'll have our answer." We do wear stubbornness like a badge of honor in my family.

Cradling my cell phone between my shoulder and ear, I hand the gate agent my boarding pass and file down the jetway stifling the urge to run. This year the fates swirled and conspired against our annual mother/sister week in Florida. My house in California sold before it hit the market. I needed to be packed and waving goodbye to the moving van in only three weeks.

A normal person would have cancelled the trip. Obviously I'm not normal. To my credit or discredit, you be the judge, I honor all my commitments, AT ALL COSTS! Even with a mountain of moving chores ahead of me, a part of me needed to escape, and that part smiled as I boarded the plane. "They'll just have to finish the week without me."

"I gotta go mom. They're closing the plane door and I need to turn my phone off." As I'm hanging up, I hear her quiet "I love you."

Ahhh, 30,000 feet in the air, off the grid, no one can call me, LET ALONE call me "Baby!"

It's been said that I was a difficult child from the get-go, a breach baby born early. Family lore has it I stuck my foot out of my mom's vagina while she was peeing. It's not glamorous, I know. I figured I must have had a clue what I was in for and was trying to get the hell out of Dodge.

In the mommy lottery, I got the one that seemed ticked off by life. Tempers flared and angry words flew throughout our household. I survived mostly by adopting a Teflon strategy of convincing myself that nothing could stick to me.

We all tiptoed around my mother because we knew that the slightest thing could provoke a tornado-like rage, and leave a mile-wide path of destruction in its wake. Yes, in our house we got daily reminders of why they name hurricanes after women. No wonder I resist being called Baby. I learned early on to depend on myself, to be nobody's baby.

Anne Lamott says that "Forgiveness is giving up all hope of having had a better past." When I left home, I vowed not to dwell on the past. But I quickly learned that without true forgiveness, the past would dwell in me.

With a reluctant grind, the landing gear lowers and after a couple of quick bounces the nose of the plane decides to stay connected to the runway. "Welcome to Houston" the flight attendant says.

Absentmindedly, I turn on my phone which immediately begins ringing. It's my mother shooting rapid-fire questions. "How was your flight? Where are you in the airport? How long is your layover? Did you get something to eat?" My answers are blunt and brief. My mother registers the rebuke. "I just like to know what you're doing" she sighs.

"I noticed" I say through clenched teeth.

"And you love that" she says.

"Oh, you noticed, too" I say.

Now we both laugh. It's our laughter that breaks the spell. It's what bonds us.

"Hey Mom... I love you." I say.

"Thanks Baby" she says. I take a deep breath and decide to let that one slide.

BURIED TREASURE

For years I've been considering throwing out my old journals.
Mostly because they don't reflect who I am now
And I don't want anyone reading them after I die.

A friend said "What if you get amnesia?"
I said "I think you watch too many soap operas."
No one I know has ever gotten amnesia.

Another friend suggested I name a journal buddy.
Someone tasked with showing up after I die to destroy them.
I decided to do it now, myself.

I spent several weekends going through my old journals.
Tearing out the pages I wanted to keep.
The creamy centers of my life so far.

Doing that, I uncovered two priceless emails from my mom written in 2009,
The year we couldn't fly home from California to Ohio for Christmas.
My mom always depended on me to help her create the perfect Christmas.

My favorite part of these emails is the subject line.

December 18, 2009, 3:14 pm
Subject: omg

Hi Honey,

Just got rested up from shopping. I don't think I ever realized just how much you help me and keep me centered. The weatherman predicted 2-3 inches of snow tomorrow. I REALLY MISS YOU! BUT MAYBE THIS IS A LESSON FOR ME...I AM TOO OLD FOR THIS. Merry f---------- Christmas and lots of love MOM.

December 18, 2009, 3:39 pm
Subject: disregard
Hi again,
Thought I'd better add a little to my last message. Things are going pretty good...my mood could improve a bit, don't you think?? It isn't as bad as it sounds and I am enjoying the F------ Christmas...just couldn't resist the f--- part. Love and miss you, MOM.
P.S. Are you sure you like my e-mails (Haha)

Had I not been unearthing 40 years of ramblings looking for the gems that really mattered,
I would have missed these "not to be missed" notes from my mom.

At 86 with a failing memory, my mom probably won't remember these emails
But still drops her share of f-bombs.

I hope I get a chance to visit her again.
To share them with her and tell her
Just how f------ much she and they mean to me.

PERFECTLY IMPERFECT

According to my journals our mother/sister annual vacations were torture and always ended badly, most of the time with me losing it.

By day five, I could no longer self-edit and the truth bombs began to fly.

It could be politics, life dramas that followed my sister, or the weight of making all the decisions, something would happen and my powder keg would detonate.

Once I had to leave early to go back to California and I swear they couldn't even figure out where to go to dinner.

Those times were flooded with "shoulds" for me. My (now diabetic) mom shouldn't take a second or third trip to the fudge shop. Should we buy souvenirs? My older sister shouldn't complain about my snoring. She snores, too.

Every year, I vowed never again, and when the next year rolled around, I went. The point was to travel together with mom, now that dad was gone.
It meant the world to her.

One year, she was recovering from shingles and still went.
All week long, she'd say "I'm going to go read for a little while."

And we would find her two minutes later, book in her hand, asleep in her bed.

Lately, pictures from those trips flash up on my screen.
The emotions that flood me don't match the story I just told.
I don't see only the hardness of it all although at times it was difficult.

I see us, partnered at the kitchen table playing Canasta until the wee hours.
I see us finding a seat close enough so mom can hear the ocean while we take a walk.
I see us on the beach, toes buried in the warm sand, usually drink in hand, waiting for a special sunset.

I see us together.
Perfectly imperfect.

ZIGZAG

I'd love to meet you yesterday. Sounds like a plan. I'll wait for you by the telephone pole at the end of the driveway that used to be base for our after dark games of Hide and Seek. Don't worry if you are late, I can catch fireflies and put them in the jar I poked small holes in with the point of the can opener. When we're done, I'll walk you halfway home and then you can walk me halfway home over and over because that's what good friends do. It's best we don't bother my mother. She will most likely be inside smoking Virginia Slims and eating candy from the stash she keeps hidden from us in her bedroom drawer. Let's try to avoid my brother and sister, too. It won't be hard to do. My dad won't come home for hours, probably not before I go to bed but I know he loves me.

I've been saving my babysitting money for a coat I saw at Zayre's. Mom says we can't afford it but I'm going to try to find a way to get it because I love how flashy it is. I hate piano lessons. What a waste of a $1.50. Mrs. Simpson spends most of her time smacking my hands while telling me to curve my fingers and asking me why can't I be more like my sister Terry. I don't tell her it's because Terry has few friends. Maybe Friday we can go to the playground recreation thing and make more lanyards. What are we going to do with all those lanyards? Let's ride our bikes and cut through the National Guard Army Reserve Center again.

Blackie had more kittens today. I hope I get to keep one this time. My dad doesn't like cats very much. On the weekends he would probably notice if I try to keep the gray one. My mom lets me mash potatoes for dinner now. I eat a bunch while I'm mashing them on the dryer behind the back door where the mixer sits.

Sheri Luft's mom makes homemade cookies and all her clothes. I think it's cool; Sheri hates it. Her mom is going to teach me to sew that is after I take the bus downtown to Woolworth's and buy the pattern and fabric. It's gonna be really cool. Her brother is away at Kent State, the college where the National Guard killed those students protesting the Vietnam War.

Flash forward…Sheri went to college, and teaches in the same school as her mother, or at least she did, until the day her brother murdered her, her mother and father. They say the voices told him to do it. Some things can't be fixed but luckily the sleeve I sewed inside out three times as Mrs. Luft patiently taught me to sew could.

ABOUT THIS POEM

This poem, inspired by David Jordan's *Let's Meet Yesterday*, provides enough details to imagine my late 60s early 70s childhood. I still remember how Sheri rolled her eyes every time I came to her house for a sewing lesson. Senior year, we worked on yearbook staff together. She appeared often in the pages, most times dressed in my outfits. Sheri was a bridesmaid in my February 1972 wedding, wearing a red velvet, empire waist dress, trimmed in white lace. She lived a rather ordinary life until an extraordinary tragedy. Side note: My father made sure my mom could buy that coat for me. I loved clothes so much my mother always said "you spend your life in layaway waiting for payday."

NO REGRETS

In my early writing days, I wrote more than 500 blog posts on a women's empowerment site.
I only know the number because the charismatic leader congratulated me on my contribution.
My participation came to a screeching halt after I attended an in-person event in Los Angeles.
Five minutes into the Friday night cocktail mixer,
I realized it was a cult.

"Life changing" programs were pushed hard,
Ones where they tear you down and then build you back up,
Ones costing thousands of dollars,
Ones marketed with questionable tactics,
To people who I questioned could afford them.

My spirit was crushed. How did I miss this?
After a quick call home to tell my husband the shocking news,
I returned to the mixer. Now I really needed a glass of wine.
As I began meeting and talking to other women there,
I soon realized, I was in the company of big dreamers.

Beautiful, earnest, vulnerable people hoping for and needing a break.
One particular group had a fascination with Iraqi currency.
Believing the Dinar would be revalued soon and anyone holding it would get rich.

There were plans drawn on cocktail napkins about chartering private jets to fly them to collect their enormous gains and Cayman Island banks.

They believed it so much, I wanted to believe it, too.
Not the private jet part that was crazy.
The part where this could happen for them.
That they could finally step away from the financial cliff that was making the draw to the flame so irresistible.

I may or may not have some Iraqi Dinar tucked away in a drawer that didn't live up to its promise…yet.
My pay to play was a small wager that luckily I could afford.
My reward, standing in the company of believers the likes of which I had never met before.
Priceless!

KNOWING

One day, I will wake up and wish for nothing and say thank you for everything.
Even the things I cried over, the things that ended, the things I sat down.
I will say "thank you for leaving me to find my right way."

One day, I will breathe into the deepest caverns of my being.
Knowing, I kept the best parts, the ones that were mine to keep.
Knowing, I let everything else drop to the ground, to find its own home.

One day, I will honor the miracle of finding my true self.
Because today, I realized there is only thing I can't live without.
Knowing the "real me."

FINDING OUR WAY HOME

The feet find their way by feeling.
Feeling roots barely above ground.
Some rough, with knob-like obstructions.
Some tripping us, blocking the path.
That leads to our grounding expanse.

The heart must find its own music.
Not the easiest one to play.
Or the one it always frequents.
One just beyond our fingertips.
Waiting for us to hear its song.

Spirit leads the feet and the heart.
Some steps are taken some are not.
Some songs sung others left behind.
We rise anew, begin again.
Finding our way home to ourselves.
In the silence and noise of life.

POSTSCRIPT

Originally, 2020 was the year scheduled for my Rumspringa. A Rumspringa (running around) is an Amish rite of passage during adolescence. It involves more freedom, greater social activity, and going on their own into the outside world.

I'm not Amish but I grew up in Ohio, the state with the largest Amish population in the country. Over 60,000 Amish live there. I always got a little chuckle when I'd hear about a Rumspringa gone awry on the television news.

After all I'd been through in 2018 and 2019, I thought I deserved one. I was ready to jump out there, be in the world with friends, take trips, celebrate life, and make up for lost time.

Then came 2020 and Covid-19. I felt a little Amish-ish during the pandemic having to stay home all the time, isolate myself from other people, and make all my own food (seriously no restaurants or bars).

I feel I've earned a Raging Rumspringa now! I'm penciling one in for summer 2021, just after V-day (Vaccination Day). Keeping my fingers crossed that it will be epic and not epidemic like last year.

PROFESSIONS OF GRATITUDE

Friends have always been an important part of my life. I'm fortunate to share in the community of many groups of talented writers and artists. Údar Anam Cara (Gaelic for Soul Friend) is a special group of poets who encourage and celebrate each other's gifts and talents. This collection of poems and essays largely came about because of their continuing love and support. Thank you all!

Laurie Marks Wagner, being a part of your Wild Writing Family at 27 Powers helped me create a solid writing practice. Many gems were created and mined from the process of Wild Writing. Thank you for all the ways you inspired me and so many other writers.

A special shout out to Mary Anne Radmacher for encouraging me and my writing for over ten years. She knew I had talent even before I did. I'm so happy to have her as a mentor and so proud to call her my friend.

Barbara Grassey, thank you for your ninja editing skills. Having an editor who believes in and loves your writing is such a gift. I couldn't have found a better partner for this project.

To the countless others who made suggestions and pointed me in the direction I needed to go to make this dream a reality, thank you.

Thanks to my family! My son Matt and "grands" Sophia and Sam, you give my life joy and meaning. Miriam, I have so much love and admiration for you. After the real hurricane and the personal hurricanes, you stepped in and soon became an important part of our family. To my extended family who I write openly and often about, I love you all! And the biggest THANK YOU saved for my husband Bob Albers, my rock for over forty years. Thank you for not dying. You have loved and encouraged me even beyond my wildest dreams. Thank you for that and so much more.

Early on in the pandemic, I realized that writing would help keep me grounded and sane. In the past, I have written myself through big events like my husband's cancer diagnosis, always reflecting the truth and tenderness of my experience. I write as a way of condensing my history into just enough words or narrative to evoke a time and place memory, on the page, and in my heart.

Writing this book has been such a joy because even in the darkest of times, I find humor. I find corners of belonging and deep knowing that uplift me. I hope as my reader, they uplift you, too.

POET

Caren Albers, author of *Happiness Junkie* and *Married to a Vegan*, writes with honesty, compassion, insight and humor. Her words can tug on your heart and make you laugh at the same time. Her quick wit and insatiable interest in irony make her writing entertaining and enlightening.

Find out more at carenalbers.com.

Made in the USA
Columbia, SC
07 April 2021

35776911R00083